D1411623

Design by Elizabeth Woll

Published by The C.R. Gibson Company
Made in the U.S.A.
ISBN 0-8378-9857-9
GB645

Our Lives Were Meant to be Shared

photographs by
Kim Anderson

poetry by Paula Finn

THE C.R. GIBSON COMPANY NORWALK, CONNECTICUT

I know you'll understand
how inadequate words are
to describe the joy and wonder
I feel about us.

When I try to define the
        special meaning
you've added to my life—I can't.
So I'll just say "thank you"...
I know you'll understand.

*Y*ou make the difference between
    feeling lost,
and feeling at home...
between listening to my fears,
and following my heart...
between having to play a role,
and feeling free to be myself...
between giving up on my problems
and giving them another try.

*I*t's such a comfort to know
that whenever the stress and demands
of the outside world get us down,

we can count on each other's warmth
and support
to help build us back up.
We're there for each other
through the highest and lowest of
times,
applauding success,
and easing the pain of defeat;
sharing the magic of each other's
dreams...
and working together to make them
come true.

We enjoy an ease of relating
that lets us be completely ourselves.
When we open up to reveal
our innermost thoughts and secrets,
we can trust each other
to treat them with care.

We realize that things
won't always go our way,
and when we give in a little more than
        we'd like
it's not a defeat
but an investment—
and we know that in choosing to share
        our lives . . .

sometimes we'll have to give up
a little more of ourselves...
to gain so much more together.

You share my joy in the good
    times
and help me to see the humor
in the bad times.
Your support makes everything a little
    easier —
And that makes a big difference.

You listen sensitively enough
    to really hear me,
you look deeply enough
    to really see me,
and you always make time
to make me feel worthwhile.

You're my best friend—
I can trust you
to show me patience
when the world is too demanding,
acceptance
when others are judgmental,
loyal support
when others turn away.

I wish that you could know
what strength I draw
from the closeness we share...
the trust I feel
when I look into your eyes...
the comfort I feel
when I hear your voice...
the happiness I know
whenever I am with you.

I wish that I could somehow
        repay you
for the gifts that have made my life
        complete…
the warmth of your companionship,
the depth of your understanding,
the constancy of your support.
You ask nothing of me,
yet nothing I could ever give you
could ever be too much.

I don't often communicate
how much your support does for me...

that yours is the stability
that calms me in times of confusion,
the comfort that eases my
        deepest sorrows,
or the encouragement that so often
makes the difference
between giving up
and giving my all.

I don't often express
how great a difference you always
      make
by offering me open arms
when I need to be held,
a listening ear
when I need to be heard,
your self—
when I need to feel loved.

So what better way to thank you
simply for being
the most important person in my life—
for you've done more for me
than anyone else has . . .

and you mean more to me
than anyone else will.

*W*hen I am stubborn
you see behind the charades
I sometimes play,
and gently push me
toward the person I'd rather be...

When I am frightened,
your comfort tells me what
I need to hear most:
I'm not alone.

When I am hurting,
I need to be reminded of the
pain my struggles create in you
for I am not used to having someone
     care so much
about me
that my suffering becomes theirs.

Your support means a lot ...

Your love means everything.

*I*t's comforting to know
we can count on each other

to understand our most complex ideas,
and to share our deepest feelings...
that we can talk openly
and trust that our words won't be
        judged.

Our communication is easy,
nourishing
and complete.

$\mathcal{M}$y wishes for us...

that we'll continue to share new
        interests and adventures,
and allow each other freedom
to develop as individuals as well...

that our faith won't be shaken by
occasional feelings of hurt or anger—
that we'll continue to acknowledge
our differences openly,
and to see them as opportunities
        to learn
and to grow closer...

that we'll find in each disagreement
the patience to listen,
the courage to trust,
and the strength to forgive.

We'll never forget
the qualities that first attracted us
    to each other
and how much we still
    appreciate them...

We'll always inspire
the best in each other,
applauding successes,
nurturing strengths—

believing in each other's dreams
and working as one to make them
come true.

We don't know
what changes lie ahead,
or where our shared path will lead...

But what I do know
is that I'm here for you today—
to listen or talk,
to applaud or console...
to want, need,

...and to love you with all my heart.